The Churches and 'Race'

A Pastoral Approach

David Haslam

Minister, Herne Hill United Church and
Christ Church East Dulwich, London

GROVE BOOKS LIMITED
RIDLEY HALL RD CAMBRIDGE CB3 9HU

Contents

Acknowledgements

My thanks go to the Grove Pastoral series editorial group, in particular Mike Booker, who offered many helpful suggestions, and also Bev Thomas of Evangelical Christians for Racial Justice and Revd Lakshme Deshpande of Nottingham University who read the text with a critical eye. Any imperfections are, however, my own responsibility.

The Cover Illustration is by Peter Ashton

Copyright © David Haslam 2001

First Impression March 2001
ISSN 0144-171X
ISBN 1 85174 458 4

1
Introduction

Life in Britain is changing, as in all the countries of Europe. We are becoming more diverse societies. Many would say we are the richer for it. It leads to some interesting experiences. As a white man whose daughter had married an African said recently, 'I found myself one of only six white people in a very large family celebration. It felt quite strange.' Someone else remarked, 'I have to pass the Mosque, the Hindu Temple and the Sikh Gurdwara now on my way to church.' Two brief stories illustrate the opportunities and challenges.

In an urban parish the church leaders were bemoaning the fact that there were too few people in the church community with potential leadership skills. On being told there were two quite senior managers working for international companies who had been attending for some time, and who might be approached, they expressed incredulity. The two were black. No-one had thought to ask them their background, or discover what gifts or experience they might have.

Responding to a national church survey, the secretary of a rural church had put 'Nil' in answer to a question about ethnic minorities. On checking the form the minister commented, 'There are actually two people from minorities in our church. No doubt, if I had asked, the secretary would have said she did not think of them as "minority."' Such an approach denies the history and identity of black or minority people.

'Race' and 'racism' are words that can make people anxious and defensive. While this is understandable they raise vital issues for church and society which need to be addressed in a positive way. In this booklet we seek to look at the issue of 'race' in a pastoral context, but that does not mean it will be without difficulty. Some in the minority communities have a saying, 'No gain without pain,' which could well apply to the journey along which this booklet is intended to encourage us.

First I will look at the changes in identity and culture which are taking place due to the presence in Britain of people from Asia, Africa, Latin America and the Caribbean, the 'minorities from the South.' I will examine terminology, definitions and what is meant by the rather pejorative term 'political correctness.' I will then consider wider society and the tensions and problems created by suspicion and distrust of minority communities. A discussion of prejudice and racism, and 'inclusivity and exclusivity,' in the Bible and theological reflection on the themes of justice, repentance and reconciliation. Finally I include suggestions of the response we might make, in the local church and wider church structures. This includes issues arising from the report on *Institutional Racism in the Diocese of Southwark,* to which this author contributed. Each chapter concludes with questions which are intended to stimulate group discussion.

2
Identity and Language

Who Is British These Days?

Britain has always been multicultural. Wales has long seen an emphasis on Welsh language and culture. Alastair Hunter has written about how even within Scotland multiculturalism is a fact—'Lowland Scots, aristocratic Anglo-Scots, native Celts, Orcadians.'[1] The debate on identity in Ireland continues actively. Citizens of the Commonwealth have been arriving in Britain since the 1940s and the minority ethnic population, excluding Irish, Scots and Welsh, is now at least 7%. Meanwhile, the English are trying to rediscover the meaning of Englishness.

There is a fine line between identity and nationalism. Perhaps we can usefully distinguish between xenophobia, nationalism and patriotism. 'Xenophobia' is the fear or hatred of foreigners. 'Nationalism' is a more neutral term but still carries a sense of 'my nation over against other nations.' I propose a definition of 'patriotism' as a love of one's own country, or culture, but not at the expense of, or in competition with, others. Arguably the best kind of patriots continue to love their culture as it changes and grows through interaction with the cultures of others.

Another way of describing such an approach is 'pluralist'—willing to accept, examine and debate with cultures or national identities different from our own. Kenneth Cracknell, in his essay on nationalism in *Belonging to Britain*, has written sensitively about this. He cites the dangers of seeing ourselves as 'chosen people,' and of Old Testament 'nationalism.' He distinguishes between nationalism and nationhood; there is work to be done on the nationhood of the British, as elsewhere. 'Perhaps a contribution the British might make,' he goes on, 'is to demonstrate that a rich plurality of nationhoods can and does exist' within one country.[2]

But to achieve this, the British will need to acknowledge, repent of and rise above their past. The excesses of colonialism and empire, and the atrocities of slavery, must be understood from the point of view of the victim. In this context repentance is a most important Christian doctrine, and one to which I will return.

'British' is now inclusive of African, Caribbean and Asian culture, as well as Scots, Welsh and Irish. In *Race for the Millennium* I defined the British as 'those who live or have lived in Britain and who—although in some cases having roots in or antecedents from other parts of the world—regard themselves as primarily of British social and cultural origin.'[3] Most of those 'from other parts' are from the Commonwealth countries. A good number are from different faith communities, including Muslim, Sikh, Hindu and Jewish. Some second or third generation

1 A Hunter, 'Watching from a Distance,' in Roger Hooker and John Sargant (eds), *Belonging to Britain* (London: CCBI, 1990) p 87.

2 K Cracknell, 'What is a Nation?' *ibid*, p 29.

3 D Haslam, *Race for the Millennium* (London: CHP, 1996) p 14.

Muslims, Sikhs and Hindus describe themselves as British.

All this brings complications for the indigenous British. Tariq Modood in *Not Easy Being British* feels 'British' is still closely identified with whiteness—and to some degree with Christianity—and that we need to move towards a concept of Britishness 'that is not frozen in history.'[4] Nor should it be identified with a narrow set of ethnicities such as English, Welsh, Scottish or Irish. It should highlight the common ground between us, past and present, as well as our contribution 'through our differences.' Modood argues the case for 'hyphenated identities,' including Black-British, Asian-British or African-British, a style fairly widely adopted in the United States in such forms as African-American or Asian-American. This debate became quite heated with the publication in October 2000 of the Runnymede Trust's Commission report, *The Future of Multiethnic Britain.*[5] The Commission argued for a more ecumenical understanding of 'British'; the politicians were far more cautious.

Language and Culture

We need further exploration of the words used to describe ourselves and others. However, we first need to familiarize ourselves with the meaning of culture. *The Concise Oxford Dictionary* (1976) describes culture as a 'particular form, stage or type of… civilization,' and as 'intellectual development,' that is, implying some growth or change. Culture is the psychological air we breathe. It includes our values, attitudes, language, history, music, art, literature, food, clothes, religion, arguably even our climate. This is as true in the church as anywhere else.

Language is important. It expresses our attitudes and thought-forms, and needs to be carefully monitored. 'Black' is still the most common term used to describe the minority communities from the South in the UK, although this is changing. I tend to use it still as a 'political colour,' inclusive of all non-Western Europeans and to some degree interchangeable with 'minority ethnic communities.' Some Asian people have resisted 'black' as a catch-all description, so 'Black and Asian' has become quite common. Minorities who are not from 'the South'—Cypriots, Turks, Romanians, and other smaller communities—do not normally describe themselves as 'black.' 'Ethnic minorities,' a term used by the Commission for Racial Equality (CRE), sounds slightly diminishing, suggesting a second-class status. Minorities from the South point out that in their countries white Europeans are the minority. The most acceptable general term currently seems to be 'minority ethnic communities,' who live alongside a *majority* ethnic community which is white British. This serves to emphasize that *all* of us are 'ethnic,' and that 'ethnic' should not be used as a synonym for different or exotic.

Language can have a negative effect in itself. I have written elsewhere about 'colour-coded language.'[6] The lunatic fringe in this debate can be found among

4 T Modood, *Not Easy Being British* (London: Runnymede Trust, 1992).
5 Runnymede Trust, *The Future of Multicultural Britain: the Parekh Report* (Profile, 2000).
6 D Haslam, *op cit*, p 10.

tabloids which carry stories such as school-children being banned from singing 'Baa baa black sheep.' That particular story had no factual basis, but there is a serious issue in the use of 'black' to convey a negative message. Examples are black spot, day, economy, mail and indeed sheep. 'Black' can also be purely descriptive—blackout, black eye, black coffee and so on. The lunatics appear here using the sneer of 'political correctness,' suggesting one should ask for coffee 'without milk,' rather than 'black.' The whole debate then becomes devalued.

Those who belittle the effect of language might reflect on the thoughts of a young black mother who wrote a poem *What shall I tell my Children?* She was deeply disturbed about bringing up her children in a world where 'black' usually means bad and 'white' almost always good. Rev'd Dr Michael Jagessar says that, 'the insensitive and pejorative use of the term "black" is offensive.'[7] If colour-coded language is oppressive to a minority, even only in their perception, other descriptive phrases should be found.

'Race,' Racism and Political Correctness

The debate on terminology may seem convoluted and overdone to some but language defines how we see both ourselves and others. The word 'race' itself needs to be discussed and used very carefully. It evolved at a time when some rather limited scientists began to propagate the idea there was more than one race. Along with that came the view that some races were superior to others. For Christians there can be only one race, the human race. Therefore, each time we use the term 'race' in a way which suggests there are different races, we are bordering on the blasphemous. There may be different cultures, different ethnic communities, even different peoples, but there is only one race. That is why, signalling caution and following sociologist Paul Gilroy, I ususally write 'race' in inverted commas, as in the title of this booklet.

This does not mean there is no such thing as *racism*. Racism is an ideology, a way of looking at the world, which believes there *are* different races and that some are superior to others. The simplest definition of racism is 'prejudice plus power.' Prejudice is not the main problem; what makes it destructive is the power to put that prejudice into practice. There are of course further definitions, the most important in recent times being that of *institutional racism* from the Stephen Lawrence Inquiry.

> Institutional racism consists of the collective failure of an organization to provide an appropriate and professional service to people because of their colour, culture or ethnic origin. It can be seen or detected in processes, attitudes and behaviour which amount to discrimination through unwitting prejudice, ignorance, thoughtlessness and racist stereotyping which disadvantage minority ethnic people.

7 'Words Hurt' *Reform* (United Reformed Church, May 2000).

The use of 'unwitting' allows people to realize that 'institutional racism' is not accusing people in an institutional framework of being deliberately racist in their words and actions. However, the attitudes and behaviour they manifest, the processes in which they are involved, and the results, may be.

The adjective 'racial' also needs cautious use. It can describe the actions of those who espouse the ideology of racism, even if inadvertently, as in 'racial discrimination' or 'racial harassment.' It should not imply there are separate races.

A relatively new term is 'political correctness.' Its origins appear to lie within the political right of the United States. It seems intended to undermine progressive initiatives in the fields of race, gender, sexuality and disability. A report from a 'Racial Consultants' Day of the United Reformed Church describes it as 'a term people use to dismiss the behaviour and language of justice.' Certain newspapers and political commentators take great delight in pronouncing initiatives towards equality as 'politically correct.' By definition, they imply, such initiatives need not be taken seriously.

'Political correctness' is a clever and confusing term, because there is often a grain of truth in its criticisms. It is clever because, whilst accepting in apparent seriousness that there *are* problems in our society, critics use the term to undermine proposals actually to *do* something. A classic example was the Lawrence Inquiry, where Judge MacPherson and his colleagues made some seventy recommendations. The right-wing press, while beating their breasts about police errors, vigorously attacked most of the recommendations. A *Daily Telegraph* editorial said political correctness is a greater problem for the police than racism, and pontificated, 'The number of people who have actually experienced police racism is almost certainly smaller than the number who have suffered from crimes while local policemen (*sic*) were attending racism awareness courses.'[8]

The term confuses because there can be elements in some supposedly progressive initiatives which are shallow or tokenistic. Some years ago, with much fanfare, an English local authority elected its first black mayor. Unfortunately the person was really not up to the job. The 'mayor's gaffes' were gleefully reported by those who pointed to 'political correctness' as the reason for his election, and mocked the black community. The idea of political correctness needs to be unpacked, and its meaning clarified.

Those accused of political correctness may well intend to do the right thing, but there are three dimensions to their aims. The first is *superficial correctness*, when an initiative is undertaken simply to deflect criticism. The next, more important, dimension is *justicial correctness* (a rather clumsy adjective coined by this author). An initiative exhibiting this quality will lead to a fairer, more just, situation and the disadvantaged being better and more fairly represented.

The third dimension of the term, particular perhaps for Christians or those of religious belief, is that of *theological correctness*. This means something is right and proper in the teaching of Christianity, or indeed of most faiths. The three different

8 Quoted in *CARF Magazine* (Campaign Against Racism and Fascism, April/May 1999).

dimensions may be illustrated in the 'equal opportunities' debate. For a body to adopt 'equal opportunity policies' is superficial correctness, unless such policies make a difference. To achieve justicial correctness there must be equality of outcome, demonstrated by monitoring. Theological correctness is the belief and practice that each human being is of equal worth and therefore *entitled* to an equal share.

The failure to confront racism, the undermining of equality initiatives by the jibe of political correctness, and the unwillingness to embrace a creative pluralism lead to the problems in wider society, to which we now turn.

Questions for Discussion

- What are your own origins, as far back as you know them?
- Do you know people who originated from outside Britain? Are they 'British,' in your view?
- Can a practising Muslim or Sikh be British?
- Is there really only one race—the human race—and if so should we stop talking of 'other races'?
- Has your understanding of 'political correctness' been changed by reading the above?

3
The Wider Society

'Stephen Lawrence was a martyr of our present age,' said the Rev'd Inderjit Bhogal, President of the Methodist Conference, in July 2000 at a vigil around the memorial plaque where Stephen was killed in April 1993. Stephen had not stood up for any great cause, nor particularly for his faith, but what he and his family had undergone was totally undeserved suffering, not for a cause but for the colour of his skin. We may not put it the same way as Rev'd Bhogal but it is unarguable that by their suffering the Lawrences have irrevocably changed British society, although not as quickly nor—yet—as radically as they hoped. The fall-out from Stephen's case has been extraordinary. Not only did the police fail to catch his murderers, but—because the Labour Government instituted a Public Inquiry—a high level of incompetence and institutional racism was exposed amonst the police and other institutions. It is extremely painful for Stephen's parents that his killers are still free, but this has encouraged enormous momentum for change.

Along with the need to address institutional racism revealed by the Lawrence Inquiry comes the necessity of deeper changes. In her book *True Colours* Yasmin Alibhai-Brown quotes Professor Bhikhu Parekh:

> Respect and recognition are complex concepts. They require that ethnic minorities should be accepted as fellow subjects fully qualified to speak for themselves and to participate in all decisions affecting their lives...Respect and recognition go beyond equal opportunity and call for a profound change in white society's attitudes to ethnic minorities.[9]

The church therefore needs to be addressing the effects of racism, in its own life and practice and in the wider society. It must press for 'respect and recognition,' and engage in the debate as to how these are to be brought about.

The climate for such changes is positive. The 1996/7 'British Social Attitudes' survey suggested there was strong support for anti-discrimination legislation, that there has been a sharp fall among those who would object to a minority ethnic boss and that fewer white people would object to a family member marrying a minority partner. A *Guardian* poll in February 2000 showed only 36% believed most white people would mind if a family member married a minority person, compared to 75% a few years earlier.

In *True Colours* Alibhai-Brown reports on surveys carried out by the Institute for Public Policy Research (IPPR), in work funded partly by the Churches Commission for Racial Justice (CCRJ). The IPPR reported that a 'qualitative survey,' with group discussions among white people, produced four distinct groups. There were the 'Die-hards' who would say 'I hate them, I admit it,' out of a racism arising partly from economic fear. (In a related survey 25% of white people inter-

9 Yasmin Alibhai-Brown, *True Colours* (London: IPPR, 1999) p ??.

viewed in Somerstown estate, near London's Euston station, said minorities should be sent 'home,' a third said they would vote for a 'white-interests' party). Then there were those who say 'I'm not racist *but*...' with little personal experience of minorities, and typically say 'I don't care what colour a person's skin is but they can't come over here and get more than we do.' There are the 'comfortable liberals,' well-educated but aware that the wider problem of racism is difficult to solve. Finally come the 'young optimists,' who tend to have minority ethnic friends and are instinctively anti-racist.

Areas of Prejudice

What are the main social areas where prejudice and discrimination should be addressed? The Stephen Lawrence Inquiry exposed *the criminal justice system*. It is clear *the police* need to take major steps in retraining officers at all levels, putting into place stronger disciplinary powers, recruiting actively from minority communities and seeking to promote minority officers. Churches can help by being in active dialogue with local police forces and recruiting lay visitors to police stations. They can ask how racial harassment is being tackled and whether minority officers are being recruited and retained. There are too few minority magistrates, solicitors, judges, probation officers and prison staff.

Unemployment is still two or three times higher among minorities. A number of schemes are available to stimulate employers, including the *Leadership Challenge* of the Commission for Racial Equality, the business-led *Race for Opportunity* initiative and the church-sponsored *Wood-Sheppard Principles*, named after Bishops Wilfred Wood and David Sheppard. The latter are promoted by the Race Equality in Employment Project, which urges churches both to adopt the Principles and commend them to companies with which they do business or in which they invest. The Principles require regular monitoring, to assess if there is progress in the numbers from minorities employed and the level they reach.

Everyone needs a decent *education*, and minorities should not be discriminated against. There is greater awareness in schools, especially in urban areas, but still under-achievement by many (but not all) minority children, insufficient minority teachers and a disproportionate number of black children excluded. Some educationalists say the National Curriculum is insufficiently pluralist in approaching history and culture, and that children are not yet being well-prepared to live in a multicultural society. There are, however, improvements in religious education. This is particularly important where religious or cultural discrimination is taking the place of racial discrimination. The report by the Runnymede Trust on *Islamophobia* is important in this respect.[10]

Another important area at the present time is *immigration and asylum*. Technically these are two different issues, but they are usually lumped together. Primary immigration to the UK has now ended, although in mid-2000 Government ministers admitted that the UK will need more immigrants in future. However,

10 Gordon Conway, *Islamophobia* (London: Runnymede Trust, 1997).

unless you have a very advanced skill, a close relative here or a million pounds to invest it is impossible to enter apart from seeking asylum. As walls against immigration have grown, so have the numbers trying to escape from conflict, famine and persecution.

A favourite description by media and some politicians of the majority of asylum-seekers has been 'bogus.' After vigorous campaigning that word is being used less by Government Ministers. Simultaneously the numbers of those being allowed to stay, either as full refugees or with 'exceptional leave to remain,' in 1999 was over 50%. The experience of those working with asylum-seekers is that the great majority have a case, although proof is difficult.

The *media* have to take some responsibility. Alibhai-Brown points out that newspapers often take the lead and politicians follow. Martin Linton MP in *Was it the Sun What did it?* has argued that papers create rather than reflect public opinion, by inventing stories, using emotional language like 'flooding' and 'swamping,' and refusing to tell the truth.[11] Protesting at the media's more outrageous misrepresentations is a thankless but essential role.

Finally, we need to think globally. Many from the South attempt to come to the West because we are wealthy. The main reason for that is because we have organized the world thus. In this post-colonial era poor countries are repaying debts they have often already repaid, and transnational companies pay the minimum of tax, buy up the elite in developing countries, and ignore the 80% who are of no interest because they have no money to spend. These issues should be of particular concern to the church as we ourselves are a part of a global family.

There are positive aspects for the poor in 'globalization,' the processes by which the barriers between countries and continents are rapidly being dismantled. The churches need to campaign actively for a more human globalizing process. There is a fundamental racism at the heart of a world in which the wealthy, powerful countries are largely white, along with Japan, and the poor, relatively powerless countries are black and brown. The underlying ideology is that they are poorer because they are less mentally capable, do not work hard enough, do not feel the hardships and do not really appreciate the better things of life. Without such a racist ideology how could we cope intellectually with the enormous differentials in our world? This is the same racism that supported the slave trade. If certain people are seen as inferior, exploitation can be justified.

Questions for Discussion

- What if anything do you think the Stephen Lawrence Inquiry has changed?
- What are the 'racial issues' in your local community?
- What can be done for asylum seekers? Is dispersal the right policy?
- Should churches speak out more on issues of 'race' and ethnicity? If so what should we say?
- What concerns should the church have about the process of globalization?

11 Martin Linton, *Was it the Sun What Did it?* (UK: Nuffield College, 1995).

4
'Race' in the Bible

The Bible manifests a constantly developing understanding of who are God's people. Alongside the calling of a special people to be God's own, there is a growing sense that God is the God of all. In some places exclusivity, even superiority, is the dominant motif; in others it is universality. In the New Testament we find Jesus constantly challenging the exclusive approach of the religious authorities and redefining the role of the people of Israel. His mesage is that all will be welcome as members of the new community of the people of God.

The Law and the Prophets

There is only space to look briefly at the Pentateuch, then at Isaiah and thirdly at the fifth-century (BCE) debate between what I term the 'exclusivists,' Nehemiah and Ezra—who see the Hebrews as God's chosen and only people—and the 'inclusivists,' the writers of Ruth and Jonah—who have a wider view of God's concerns. In the five books of the Law Israel is frequently told to treat aliens, foreigners and strangers as they would expect to be treated, (for example Exodus 22.21, Exodus 12.43ff, Leviticus 19.9–10 and 33–34, Deuteronomy 10.18–9, 23.7–8 and 29.10f).

In Isaiah a progression can be observed from a rather self-obsessed view of the nation to a wider view. Most scholars accept the book of Isaiah develops through three sections. The first part (chapters 1 to 39) is usually dated between about 740 and 700 BCE, and the next 15 chapters during the exile, 587 to 540 BCE. The final 11 chapters relate to the post-exilic period when the people were seeking to rebuild their community. A more inclusive approach develops as we move through the book. The writer in the earlier part of Isaiah is largely concerned with the internal affairs of the nation. Outsiders enter into it mostly when they are used as a threat, such as when God describes the Assyrian as 'the rod I wield in my anger,' or in 34.2 and 37.36.

In chapters 40–55 there is a less hectoring approach. The tone is gentler, the people are oppressed and far from home. The prophet refers to 'coasts and islands' suggesting his message is for a wider audience. He evolves the idea of the servant, the one who suffers, for his own people and beyond, and who will also bring justice (see 42.4). Cyrus, the Persian king, can be God's anointed (45.1) and God will strengthen him so that, 'from east to west all may know there is none beside me.' Finally Israel may become a light to the nations. This will remain true even when the servant people is rejected, and undergoes suffering (chapter 53).

The third section of Isaiah makes it—slightly patronizingly—clear that 'foreigners' are acceptable, for example 56.5–7, which concludes, 'my house will be called a house of prayer for all nations.' (Interestingly Matthew has Jesus quoting this verse as he cleanses the Temple in 21.13, with the last three words omitted.)

There follow directions in chapters 58 and following as to how God's people should live, to become a light to all nations.

Inclusive or Exclusive?

The argument over inclusivity reaches its zenith in the debate between the writers of Ezra and Nehemiah and those of Ruth and Jonah. Most scholars now believe these books were all produced in their final form after the Exile, in the second half of the fifth or first half of the fourth century. Nehemiah is primarily an exclusivist, although in chapter 2 it is the Persian king who releases him to rebuild Jerusalem, and provides the materials for reconstruction. The work begins but is ridiculed by non-Israelites Sanballat, Tobiah and Geshem (2.19). Nevertheless the rebuilding is completed and the people gathered together for the reading of the Law (8.1).

In 9.2 the Israelites confess their wickedness in mixing with foreigners. In 13.8 Nehemiah evicts Tobiah from his Temple room. In 13.23f Jews who have married women from Ammon and Moab are made with threats and beatings to swear they will end intermarriage. When Nehemiah discovers the high priest's son has married Sanballat's daughter, he drives him away (13.28). The vulnerability of the post-exilic community may offer some explanation for their negativity.

But Ezra takes even fiercer action against intermarrying Jews. In chapter 10 he gathers all the men in front of the Temple. He demands they make confession to God, and cut themselves off from 'foreign wives.' In a form of 'ethnic cleansing' the men agree, and the women and children are 'dismissed,' whither we know not. By tradition, the Samaritans were descended from these intermarriages.

The stories of Ruth and Jonah in their different ways challenge these views. Ruth is a Moabitess, deeply committed to Naomi, her Hebrew mother-in-law. She leaves her people to care for Naomi in her lonely old age. As luck would have it however, in 'Mills and Boon' manner, Ruth apparently seduces Naomi's kinsman Boaz, and he marries her. The story's point emerges when, apparently, from this 'mixed marriage' is descended King David himself.

Jonah is quite different from the other 'minor prophets.' Although Jonah is sent to 'Nineveh' the story was very likely written long after Nineveh was destroyed. As he flees from God's call the 'foreign' sailors try to save the ship, but eventually throw him overboard. When Jonah finally preaches to the wicked Ninevites they repent and—to his chagrin—escape punishment. Jonah is more concerned about a dying plant than the thousands of Nineveh. The tale seems an ironic message to Jews who denied that God was God of all.

There was great suspicion between Samaritans and Jews after the fourth century BCE. The Samaritans built their own temple at Mount Gezirim. By Jesus' time they seemed to have been regarded by the Jewish religious leadership as 'aliens.' The gospel writers, however, seem to see Jesus as inclusive, following the tradition of Ruth and Jonah.

For example, John 4 tells the story of Jesus and the Samaritan woman. Their exchange raises issues of both race and gender. They discuss the relative merits of

Mount Gezirim and Jerusalem, Jesus suggests that in him the traditions are drawn together. The time has come for Jews and Samaritans to worship together 'in spirit and in truth.' The woman calls on everyone to 'come and see.' The underlying message is Jesus is Messiah for all. This is underlined by the occasions when Jesus shares a meal-table with 'sinners' (Mark 2.15) and those not observing Jewish cleanliness rituals (Mark 7.1f).

Luke refers to a number of incidents involving Samaritans. In chapter 10 comes the story of the (so-called) Good Samaritan. Its fundamental point is not that the needy by the roadside should be helped but that the one who acted as a 'neighbour' was a hated Samaritan. The adversarial lawyer apparently cannot bring himself to name the benefactor's ethnic origin, responding to Jesus' question as to the man's identity (through clenched teeth?) with, 'the one who showed him kindness.' In Luke 17 only the Samaritan of the ten lepers returns to thank Jesus.

Most revealing of all is Jesus' response in John 8.48 to the accusation that he himself was a Samaritan, and is possessed. He denies he is possessed, but does not deny the charge of being a Samaritan. Finally, in an encounter where Jesus seems to learn a great deal, he is challenged by a Syro-Phoenician woman (Mark 7.25–30). Not only does this Gentile come to him for help, she deflects his brutal rejection with a humble yet deeply challenging reply, 'Even the dogs under the table eat the children's scraps.' You can almost hear Jesus's 'Ouch!' He tells her that her daughter is healed. She has been invited to the table.

Other biblical passages worth discussing include Paul in Galatians 3 and Peter's vision in Acts 10. The struggles in the Early Church over the acceptance of Gentiles are significant, not least because most of us are Gentiles and should be grateful to Paul and others who argued for Gentile inclusion. There was, therefore, a battle throughout the Old Testament, extending into the New, between those who took a narrow view of which 'race' God was interested in, and those with wider vision. Jesus was clearly one of the latter. The table is for all.

Questions for Discussion

- Does it help to try and relate what the Bible teaches to the world of today, in the field of 'race' and ethnicity? How?
- Do you have any sympathy with the position of Ezra and Nehemiah?
- Do you have another interpretation of Ruth or Jonah?
- Are there 'Samaritans' in our situation today?
- What did Jesus learn from the Syro-Phoenician woman? What might she have to teach us?

5
Theological Reflections

How do we respond theologically? What is our praxis—'thought plus action'—going to be? What are the fundamental issues, for if theology is not 'thought plus action' about fundamental issues is it not irrelevant? The key areas which must be addressed are justice, repentance and reconciliation.

Let us consider these topics in the context of a theological approach I term 'struggle.' I have written elsewhere that this is not a common theological category, and some might argue it is not a theological category at all. I believe, however, that unless theology helps in envisioning how things might be better, and then moving towards them, it is largely wasted. Struggle 'suggests effort, it implies resistance against that effort, but it also carries the connotation of movement, of progress' that eventually may achieve, although not without cost.[12]

Justice

Justice is one of the most profound biblical concepts. It is like an unbreakable cord running through both the Bible and Christian theology, the steel frame which reinforces already heavy concrete, the diamond whose cutting power against other surfaces is supreme. Justice, or 'righteousness' as it appears in older translations, is a constant theme through the law, the prophets, the psalms and the gospels. Other biblical teaching has always to be tested against it.

In Deuteronomy, in the 'Song of Moses,' Israel is told that all God's ways are just (32.4). Moses requires the people to appoint officers and judges who will seek 'justice and justice alone' (16.18–20). Finally, says Moses, the people will only live long if their weights and measures are 'true and correct' (25.15). If the people of God want to remain his people, justice must be at the heart of their dealings with one another.

As we have seen above, in Deuteronomy and Leviticus the law requires the people of God to treat strangers and foreigners in the same way as they treat one another. The book of Job struggles with the problem that life is often harder for the just. The Prophets constantly remind the people of God's obsession with righteousness, for example Jeremiah 12.1, Amos 5.24, Micah 6.8 and Zechariah 7.9.

In the teaching of Jesus, love tends to be regarded as the centre of the gospel message. However, commentator Ched Myers argues that what Jesus was about was actually constructing a new socio-economic order, based on equality and justice. He says in *Binding the Strong Man* that the feeding of thousands in the wilderness is basically about the need to share. Jesus assesses the resources, divides the people into groups, gives a blessing and proceeds with the distribution. The miracle here, says Myers, 'is the triumph of the economics of sharing within

12 D Haslam, *op cit*, p 152.

a community of consumption over against the economics of autonomous consumption in the anonymous marketplace.'[13]

Myers goes on to argue that Jesus' commitment to justice is so strong he is struggling to set up an alternative economic structure which comes to fruition in Acts 2.42–47. The rich young ruler is an archetype for those living unjustly. In the original version preserved by Mark, Jesus adds to the commandments one more, 'do not defraud,' which both Matthew and Luke omit. By definition, a rich man's wealth has been gained by defrauding the poor and a camel can pass through a needle's eye more easily than a rich man entering God's kingdom (Mark 10.25). According to Myers, for Jesus 'the *only* way to salvation for the rich is by the redistribution of their wealth—that is, the eradication of class oppression.'[14]

That of course involves struggle and pain. Justice for all is essential, within the church, in our society and in the global economy. A commitment to racial justice is a vital component of the commitment to justice as a whole, but there will be a cost.

Repentance

This is the usual translation of the Greek *metanoia*. However, the Greek word is more dynamic—it implies action, a turning away from sin, from rebellion against God towards what is right. It is a concept that needs to be addressed at individual and at corporate level. The story of the rich young ruler is again used, this time by the black American theologian James Cone, to show the white church must be willing to ask, 'What must I do to be saved?' If that question is asked seriously, says Cone, and the answer acted upon, there is hope for forgiveness.[15]

A process is outlined here, and built on more fully in the final chapter. It is crucial to listen to what black and minority Christians might be saying to us. Sometimes we may have to listen quite hard, either because they are speaking softly, due to previous reactions, or they have grown tired and now only repeat such things occasionally.

In researching the Southwark Diocese report (see next chapter), it was noticeable that—despite the presence of two black members on the inquiry panel—it took time for minority people to believe the inquiry was serious in wanting to hear from them. John Wilkinson, an Anglican priest who worked for many years in inner-city Birmingham, says black people have evolved a 'survival theology,' to enable them to get by in white ecclesiastical institutions. However, they are now discovering a liberation theology which challenges whites to repentance.

Black British theologian Robert Beckford emphasizes this in *Jesus is Dread*. He reminds us there is now a black church in the UK, and that its people have a different perspective from minority people in the 'traditional' churches. He says that, as a black Pentecostal Christian, he wants to move 'from cultural resistance

13 Ched Myers, *Binding the Strong Man: A Political Reading of Mark's Story of Jesus* (New York: Orbis, 1988) p 206.
14 Ched Myers, *op cit*, p 275.
15 James Cone, *Black Theology and Black Power* (New York: Seabury, 1969) p 81.

to culture as liberation.' He notes there is a language in the black churches he calls 'black-talk,' and from that talk he chooses the term 'Dread' to exemplify what he means by black liberation. Politically, he says, 'Dread is concerned with rebellion.' Theologically, 'to talk of a Dread Christ points us to a Christ of faith who participates in the struggles for black freedom.'[16]

White Christians need to enter into genuine dialogue with minority Christians. This will help us to turn away from racism, from the need for domination, from belief in our cultural superiority, towards what is right. As American Methodist Joe Agne says, we need to become 'recovering racists,' never claiming 'I am not racist.'[17] If we are actively engaged in the struggle, says Agne, sometimes black people may feel able to say to us, 'You seem to be overcoming your ancestral racism.'

There is also a place for public apology, for corporate repentance, regarding both the past and the present. There were a number of limited apologies by political leaders in the approach to the Millennium, including by Bill Clinton for slavery and Tony Blair for some of Britain's activities in Ireland. The Pope also acknowledged that the Roman Catholic Church had fallen short in a number of areas. The churches seem to find it difficult to recognize publicly our failures regarding racism and slavery. There is a resistance to repentance for things for which we disclaim direct responsibility. But in the case of slavery, colonialism and racism the effects, including the continuing economic benefits, remain with us today. The industrial revolution was built partly on capital from the slave trade. Africa in particular still suffers gravely from economic neo-colonialism. The effects of racism are spread across five continents and undergird contemporary monetary imperialism. Heartfelt apologies would therefore seem appropriate, given some of the things we now know about church collusion in slavery, its ideology of racism and the ongoing effects. Saying sorry, at local or international level, is extraordinarily helpful for renewing relationships, for reconciliation—individually and collective—and for fresh commitment to tackle economic injustice.

Reconciliation

This becomes possible when repentance is real. My experience is that people from Asia, Africa and the Caribbean are only too ready to forgive when Europeans demonstrate true repentance. The recent history of Zimbabwe may have obscured the memory of a people who allowed into a liberated Parliament men who were responsible for the deaths of thousands of their fellow Africans. There is a similar story in South Africa. Most African-Americans manifest their approach to reconciliation through a warm willingness to work with white people who demonstrate their repentance by engaging in dialogue and the struggle for change.

16 Robert Beckford, *Jesus is Dread* (London: Darton, Longman, Todd, 1998), p 146.
17 Joe Agne, 'Moving Deeper to the Connective Tissue: Christian Response to Hate Violence,' unpublished paper, 1989, p 5.

I used to have on my car's back window a sticker saying 'God is Black.' It occasioned some anguish among church members, but in terms of ability to forgive and be reconciled I believe it to be true. The grace and mercy of African, Caribbean and Latin American people, which often springs from an enduring Christian faith, is a blessing which makes reconciliation possible.

One obstacle in this process is the defensiveness which bedevils so many white responses to suggestions of racism. In the work both during and after the Southwark Inquiry there was a marked difference between white people who accepted the general thrust of our work—while debating particular issues of concern—and those who persistently resisted our conclusions.

Whites need to be engaged in anti-racist struggles in partnership with, and preferably under the leadership of, minorities themselves. That is not to say that all members of minority ethnic communities are always right. But if we follow the steps through the process of repentance, and if we too are seen to be suffering—even just a little—for our stance against racism, new relationships are on offer and new beginnings can be made.

Questions for Discussion

- Is justice as important to Jesus as love?
- What is your church doing, locally or nationally, to help create racial justice? What else could it do?
- Have white European Christians genuinely repented of the mistakes of the past, including slavery, colonialism and racism?
- Have any in your group suffered as a result of racism (that is, prejudice plus power)?
- What more could churches do to open the way to genuine reconciliation?

6
Focus on the Church

The Southwark Report

In 1999 the Anglican diocese of Southwark asked the Commission for Racial Equality (CRE) to enquire into its 'institutional racism.' It was the diocese in which Stephen Lawrence was murdered, and the bishops rightly felt the church could not challenge the police or anyone else unless they were willing to take a hard look at the diocese itself. The Church of England had produced national reports, such as *Seeds of Hope* (General Synod, 1991) and *Passing Winter* (Church House Publishing, 1996) but this was the first detailed diocesan enquiry.

The Inquiry was chaired by Sir Herman Ouseley and the panel included this author. The report *Institutional Racism in the Diocese of Southwark* has, I hope, set a precedent for other regional church structures.[18] The panel gathered all the reports the diocese had produced, and interviewed people from the minority communities and the diocesan structures. This included the four bishops, the diocesan secretary, the diocesan Directors of Ordinands, Education, and Church and Society, archdeacons and rural deans, and advisers on lay training, rural ministry, urban projects and race relations. Southwark Diocese has had a Race Relations Commission since 1983 and, more recently, a well-attended annual Black Forum.

The Inquiry focused on the need for better representation of minorities at all levels. It was suggested to us that many attempts had been made to ensure fairer representation. But the facts were that, in a diocese with a large number of black people, and some churches with 80–90% black congregations, the proportion of black people attending Diocesan Synod was well below 10%. On bodies like the Board of Finance, the Bishop's Council Advisory Committee and the Finance and General Purposes Committee representation was nil. This was despite a Greater London minority population above 20%, rising towards 50% in some areas.

Low minority representation at the national Methodist Conference was partly resolved through a resolution which gave targets to Districts with a fair proportion of minorities. They were asked to send at least one and preferably two minority representatives. This almost doubled the representation and it has remained at that higher (though not yet fully satisfactory) level ever since.

Other initiatives suggested by the Inquiry included the need for a high-level committee in the diocese to develop a long-term programme on equal opportunities, with monitoring to gauge the rate of change and training for all those who needed it. This was to include racism awareness training for the majority community and 'empowerment' training for minorities. The role of clergy as 'gate-keepers' was felt to be particularly important. Training for them pre- and

18 *Report on an Independent Inquiry into Institutional Racism in the Diocese of Southwark* (London: Diocese of Southwark, 2000).

post-ordination is essential. Their role in encouraging minorities to seek vocations and in congregational awareness-building is vital.

Finally the Inquiry sought a fundamental change in culture for the Church of England away from its largely white, male, middle-class culture to a much more multicultural, multiethnic presence. The subtleties and time-scale of this process were recognized but the panel felt it was essential if the church is to become what it should. A wide gap has opened between the traditional churches and the younger generation in minority ethnic communities. The implications of this story from the Report should be obvious.

A group of young black people in an inner-city parish, drawn into their church by the encouragement of white clergy, said they were trying to participate more actively in church leadership. At least one was considering offering for the priesthood. Their problem, however, was that church culture was so far removed from their peers that their friends outside could not conceive how any black person could follow a vocation. If the church did not change, they could see no future in it.

No Hiding Place

The above section outlines a 'regional' church response. Most readers will not operate regionally and it is difficult to generalize about a 'local' response. There is a considerable variety of local congregations, for example the 'urban flagship,' the inner-city, the suburban, the country town and the village. There is some overlap between the categories, but these churches will have different class-bases, various proportions of minority ethnic communities and a range of theological approaches. What is no longer possible is to hide behind the mantra, 'There aren't any here,' a phrase often repeated by Christians in suburban and rural areas. Now, thanks to the Indian restaurant, the Chinese take-away and the Asian corner shop, minorities are everywhere. In many rural areas, particularly in Ireland, there are travelling people, who are also a minority ethnic community. The dispersal of asylum-seekers is adding to this trend.

In more rural areas the importance of the church which, through its posters, its newsletter and its witness can challenge people to look beyond the local, is illustrated by the following story, as well as one of those cited in the Introduction:

An Asian family took over the corner shop in a Welsh village. Before long the young men of the surrounding area were beginning to make racist remarks and gathering to taunt family members. The women of the village, annoyed with the behaviour but also realizing it could mean the loss of the shop, formed a picket line to protect the family from harassment.

Reports have been written on rural racism, such as *Keep Them in Birmingham*[19] and *Not in Norfolk*.[20] Here is a typical rural story.

19 Eric Jay, *Keep them in Birmingham* (London: Commission for Racial Equality, 1992).
20 Helen Derbyshire, *Not in Norfolk* (Norwich: Norfolk and Norwich Racial Equality Council, 1994).

In a village church a visiting minister was astonished to notice the children were still using an old missionary collecting box to put their money in. It was an African child's head from which the tongue was outstretched. When money was put on the tongue it drew the money inside. The local leaders did not see this as a problem, even were an African to attend a service.

Issues of race and ethnicity need to be tackled differently in rural, suburban and urban contexts. General guidelines follow, addressed primarily to the majority community.

Taking the Plunge

There is a good deal of anxiety and even fear about engaging with issues of ethnicity and racism. This is understandable but not constructive. It is important for white people to take courage, push off from the side and try to swim. A determined if not yet fully-informed anti-racism will act as buoyancy. The following suggest the forms anti-racism might take.

The first important step is to *listen* to what people from black and minority communities say. It is extraordinary how white people always think they know better, even than those whose experience is being discussed. Like Job's friends, white people need to sit and listen, feel the pain, and sometimes wait for quite a long time before black people are prepared to tell them how they really feel.

In a previous booklet in the Grove Pastoral series, *Better Will Come*, a number of black people were quoted as to their experiences of racism in the church.[21] One remarked that his understanding of the Fall was that he had to face racism six days a week, out in the world, he did not expect to have to deal with it on the seventh day. Another said her heart sank when a young white lad who had attended church a couple of times was invited to read a lesson when long-term black attenders were rarely offered the opportunity.

Better Will Come summarized the views of its black respondents as follows:

1. To be black in white-led churches is very painful; it is a hard struggle to keep going.
2. The pastoral needs of black Christians are not being met and the whole church is deprived of their contribution.
3. Racism is 'institutionalized' in structures and practices whereby black Christians are marginalized and rendered ineffective even if they are nominally leaders.
4. There is a 'real scandal of racism in the churches' which white Christians often deny.

The experience of the Southwark Diocesan Inquiry suggests we have not moved

21 Maurice Hobbs, *Better Will Come* (Grove Pastoral booklet P 48, 1991).

on very far.

A second guideline is to *facilitate people from minority communities in coming together*, if they wish to do so. This can be particularly true in communities where they are few. People often need mutual support to be truthful in such situations, and white people are more likely to hear what is being said if it comes from a group rather than one or two isolated individuals. It is quite extraordinary how white people who continually meet together to make decisions become greatly agitated and even threatened when black people start meeting, even simply to share experience.

It is important to *respect all cultures and neither patronize nor stereotype* minorities. Have you ever been somewhere where you have been a minority whose status and value is suspect, even your very presence? I once made the mistake on an anti-racist march of asking some young black people in a rather patronizing way where they were from. I was made to understand in no uncertain terms that they did not care to be so addressed. Treating people with respect and as equals is essential if we are to overcome past mistakes. The battle against stereotyping is a continuous one; here is another illustrative story.

> *The author of this book, moving to a new area of London, went to the local doctors' group practice to register. Seeing behind the counter two middle-aged white women talking with a young black woman, he waited till the black woman went out with some files, assuming she was a clerk. He announced himself to the receptionist and after waiting a few minutes was told the doctor was ready. Going into the room he discovered his doctor was the young black woman he assumed was there to do the filing.*

The next guideline for white Christians is to *reflect on what is being learned* from engaging in the anti-racist struggle, perhaps in a training opportunity. We white people need to acknowledge the constant struggle against racism. We are prisoners of our own culture, in which the idea of the superiority of western Europeans is all-pervasive. This informs our belief about our history, music, drama, literature, poetry and art. It is how we have been brought up, the cultural air we have breathed. It is extremely difficult to break free from the racial stereotypes we have inherited.

Perhaps the most important venture those of us who are white can make is to *seek to stand in the shoes of a minority person*. Have you ever found yourself powerless, anxious and alone? I recall arriving for the first time in Lagos airport at midnight, expecting to be met by a church representative. There had, however, been a misunderstanding, and it was only after a nervous hour of being importuned by various individuals offering conflicting advice that I took what looked a moderately reputable taxi to the church compound where I finally found a bed.

What might it feel like in our society, in our churches, to be an 'outsider'? What are the words we have heard used about such persons, on the bus, among neighbours, even in the church? How would we feel if people stereotyped or patronized us, when they do not understand our accent when we have to really concentrate to understand theirs? What is it like when whites do not think we are capable, have no idea what our experiences or qualifications might be, hang on more tightly to their wallets and handbags when we are around? Standing in the shoes of another is good, Christian, incarnational theology. It is what we believe God did for us. It is a very revealing way to try to understand what it feels like to be a member of a minority community in Britain today.

Finally, when we have taken the anti-racist plunge, what actions can we encourage to redress the discrimination and disadvantage of the past? Hopefully the above type of missionary box and other less offensive pictures and artefacts in churches have been removed. These might include paintings of a fair-haired, blue-eyed Jesus, on the grounds of falsely stereotyping a Palestinian Jew. We need to use more positive images of black and minority people, and their contributions to church and society, on our notice boards, in our newsletters, on our walls.

We should use Racial Justice Sunday, on the second Sunday in September, more effectively. Recently CCRJ has produced more material for use in towns and villages. A black preacher could be invited, with proper preparation for both parties and with opportunities for discussion. We might use a wider range of materials from different cultures in our worship, read more books by minority authors, or subscribe to the CCRJ magazine *Church and Race*. We should join campaigns, whether against the deportation of asylum-seekers, racial harassment or discrimination in the criminal justice system. We need to find out our facts, but too often the authorities' minds are only changed by active and vigorous representation. It is not enough to be non-racist; the church needs to be anti-racist. It may be more uncomfortable, and indeed more costly, but Christians should not be much surprised by that.

Questions for Discussion

- Who are the minorities in your area?
- Are they involved in the church, otherwise what contact do the churches have with them?
- Do they have a group or platform from which they can address the majority community?
- Is the church ready to hear what they might say?
- How can the church at local, regional or national level take positive action, with minorities, to ensure they can make their full contribution?

7
Useful Organizations

Churches' Commission for Racial Justice (CCRJ), Inter Church House, 35 Lower Marsh, London SE1 7RL (Tel 020 7 620 4444)

Catholic Association for Racial Justice (CARJ), 9 Henry Road, London N4 2LH (Tel 020 8 802 8080)

Commission for Racial Equality (CRE), Elliott House, 10–12 Allington St, London SW1E 5EH (Tel 020 7 828 7022)

Evangelical Christians for Racial Justice (ECRJ), c/o Brixton Baptist Church, Solon Road, London SW2 5UY (Tel 020 7 733 7754)

African-Caribbean Evangelical Alliance, 186 Kennington Park Road, London SE11 4BT (Tel 020 7 582 0228)

Race Equality in Employment Project (REEP), Christ Church, 27 Blackfriars Road, London SE1 8NY (Tel 020 7 928 3970)

Runnymede Trust, 133 Aldersgate Street, London EC1A 4JA (Tel 020 7 600 9666)